Sim, Pim and the Bat

By Sally Cowan

Sim and Pim sat.

Sip, sip!

Sim! Sim!

Is it a rat?

Sip, sip!

Pim! Pim!

Is it a cat?

Pim and Sim met a bat.

The bat is Tib.

Tib the bat
can sip and sip.

Pim and Sim can sit.

Sip, sip, sip!

CHECKING FOR MEANING

1. What sound can Sim and Pim hear? (*Literal*)

2. What is the name of the bat? (*Literal*)

3. Why do Sim and Pim meet the bat? (*Inferential*)

EXTENDING VOCABULARY

sip	Look at the word *sip*. Can you think of another word that means the same?
rat	Look at the word *rat*. What is the smaller word within the word *rat*? Can you think of other words that end in –*at*?
bat	Look at the word *bat*. What other words can you think of that rhyme with *bat*?

MOVING BEYOND THE TEXT

1. How do you think Sim and Pim feel when they meet Tib the bat?

2. Can you think of other animals that make interesting sounds?

3. What other animals live in trees?

SPEED SOUNDS

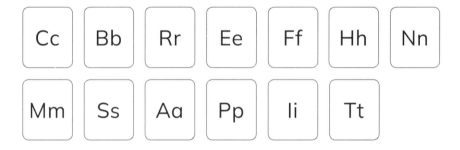

Cc	Bb	Rr	Ee	Ff	Hh	Nn
Mm	Ss	Aa	Pp	Ii	Tt	

PRACTICE WORDS

cat

rat

bat

met

Tib

can